Strength for the Struggle:
Devotional Prayers for Life's Hard Days
by
Dawn J. Douglas

TABLE OF CONTENTS

DEDICATION

INTRODUCTION

DAY 1

When You Need Healing

DAY 2

When You Feel Anxious or Overwhelmed

DAY 3

When You're Waiting on God

DAY 4

When All Your Plans Fall Apart

DAY 5

When You're Facing Financial Hardship

DAY 6

When You've Been Waiting a Long Time and the Answer Hasn't Come

DAY 7

When You Feel Alone or Forgotten

DAY 8

When You're Grieving a Loss

DAY 9

When A Friend Betrays You

DAY 10

When You Feel Unworthy or Ashamed

DAY 11

When You're Battling Depression

DAY 12

When You Need Direction

DAY 13

When God's Will Is Not What You Want

DAY 14

When You Have Irreconcilable Differences With a Family Member

DAY 15

When Your Adult Children Have Rejected You

DAY 16

When an Elderly Parent Is Facing Dementia

DAY 17

When Your Family Is Broken

DAY 18

When You're Struggling in Marriage

DAY 19

When You Must Deal With a Cheating Spouse

DAY 20

When You've Lost a Job or Opportunity

DAY 21

When You're Facing Injustice

DAY 22

When You're Afraid of the Future

DAY 23

When You Feel Spiritually Dry

DAY 24

When You're Carrying Guilt

DAY 25

When You're Under Spiritual Attack

DAY 26

When You Need Peace in the Storm

DAY 27

When You're Believing for a Miracle

DAY 28

When the Church Has Failed You

DAY 29

When Pastors Have Disappointed You

DAY 30

When You're Starting Over

DAY 31

When You Need to Remember Who You Are in Christ

BONUS DAY 1

When You Feel Invisible in Your Workplace

BONUS DAY 2

When Leadership Doesn't See Your Value

BONUS DAY 3

When You're Carrying More Than Your Share

BONUS DAY 4

When You're Tired of Fighting the System

BONUS DAY 5

When You're Trying to Lead with Integrity in a Toxic Culture

BONUS DAY 6

When You're Burdened by the Weight of Responsibility

BONUS DAY 7

When You Want to Quit but God Says Stay

BONUS DAY 8

When You're Called to Serve but Long to Be Seen

BONUS DAY 9

When You're Working Behind the Scenes but Making Kingdom Impact

BONUS DAY 10

When You're Forced to Retire with an Uncertain Future

EPILOGUE: YOU ARE STILL STANDING

BIBLE STUDY COMPANION

Reflect, Respond, and Rise Stronger in God's Word

Reflection for Any Devotional Day

Scripture Study Challenge

Group Discussion Questions

A FINAL ENCOURAGEMENT

DEDICATION

To **Trena, Tasha,** and **Fannie Mae**—
Your faith in the fire, your strength in sorrow, and your quiet endurance have inspired every line of this book. You have borne burdens that few can see, yet you continue to rise with grace and conviction. This is for every prayer you whispered in the dark, every tear you wiped in silence, and every day you chose to show up when quitting would've been easier. You are not forgotten. You are not forsaken. You are deeply seen by God.

And to every **Federal Worker** walking through uncertainty, restructuring, reduction, or retirement—
You are more than your position. Your service has mattered. Your labor is not in vain. This book was born from your struggle, your sacrifice, and your strength. May these pages remind you that even in this transition, **God is still writing your story.** The best is not behind you—it's being refined in you.

This is for the crushed.

For the courageous.

For the called.

And for every soul still holding on when the world expects them to let go.

May you find strength for the struggle—
And oil in the crushing.

INTRODUCTION

Strength for the Struggle: Devotional Prayers for Life's Hard Days

Not everyone is struggling right now. Some are in seasons of overflow, promotion, joy, and open doors—and if that's you, give thanks and dance in that season. But this book isn't written for the ones basking in breakthrough.

This book is for the ones just trying to breathe. This is for the one whose strength is nearly gone. The one whose smile hides sorrow. The one who still leads others while silently breaking down behind closed doors. The one staring at ceilings in the dark, asking God if He still hears them. The one who's still standing, but only by grace.

This is for the crushed.

Crushing is not always visible. It doesn't always come with announcements. It can look like showing up to work while carrying heartbreak. It can look like praising God while questioning His silence. It can look like faithfulness with no reward, prayer with no answer, or leadership with no support.

But here's the truth: crushing is not the end—it is where the oil flows.

In Gethsemane, Jesus was crushed. Gethsemane means "olive press," the place where pressure extracts oil. And so it is with us. Crushing in the Kingdom isn't for destruction—it's for anointing. Oil doesn't come from whole olives. It comes from what's been pressed. The same is true for your life.

If you've been in a season of disappointment, grief, betrayal, loss, waiting, or weariness—this devotional is for you. It's not filled with shallow phrases or tidy answers. It's filled with battle-tested truth. Raw prayers. Word-soaked declarations. Strength that doesn't come from this world. And hope that holds even when your hands can't.

God is not punishing you—He is purifying you.

He's not discarding you—He's distilling purpose from your pain.

You're not failing—you're being formed.

This is not your end. It's your press. And oil is coming.

These thirty-one devotions were written for the days when life feels too heavy. For the moments when you can't find the words. For the valleys that feel unending. They are prayers and reflections to hold you up when you feel like letting go.

So read slowly. Let the Spirit speak through the stillness. Cry if you need to. Pause if you must. But don't quit. Because what you're carrying isn't just pain—it's purpose being refined.

You may be pressed, but you are not crushed.

You may be struck down, but you are not destroyed.

God is still here. Still faithful. Still working.

And what's pressing you now is preparing you for power later.

This is Strength for the Struggle.

One page at a time. One prayer at a time.

Until you rise again in power.

DAY 1

When You Need Healing

The Circumstance

You're in pain—maybe in your body, maybe in your heart, or maybe in the silent battles no one can see. You've prayed. You've cried. You've waited. And still, the healing hasn't come in the way you hoped. You're worn down by the ache, and though your faith remains, it flickers in the shadow of fatigue.

Encouragement

Healing doesn't always look like we expect. Sometimes it's immediate. Sometimes it's a process. But it is always **God's desire to restore you**—to lift the weight, heal the wound, and bring you peace. Whether He heals you today, over time, or in ways deeper than you imagined, **He is with you—and He is not finished.**

Devotional Reflection

In Scripture, healing is never just physical—it's wholeness. When Jesus healed, He didn't only stop the bleeding or open blind eyes. He restored dignity. He silenced shame. He touched what others wouldn't touch. He forgave sins and called the broken beloved.

You may be asking, "God, when will You heal me?" But perhaps today He is whispering, "Let Me heal all of you."

Healing isn't just about removing pain—it's about **meeting the Healer**. His presence is the medicine, His Word the balm, and His

Spirit the breath that revives dry bones. So invite Him into every layer—body, mind, soul, and spirit. Even if your circumstance doesn't change overnight, His presence will bring peace that defies it.

You are not a burden. You are not forgotten. Your healing is held in the hands of the One who was wounded for you.

Scripture

"He was pierced for our transgressions, He was crushed for our iniquities; the punishment that brought us peace was on Him, and by His wounds we are healed."
— **Isaiah 53:5**

"Lord my God, I called to You for help, and You healed me."
— **Psalm 30:2**

"Come to Me, all you who are weary and burdened, and I will give you rest."
— **Matthew 11:28**

Prayer

Lord, my body and soul cry out for healing. I bring You the pain I can't fix and the brokenness I can't carry anymore. Heal what no medicine can touch. Reach the places no person can see. You are the God who heals, and I trust You even when I don't understand the timing. Let Your healing power flow through every part of me—physically, mentally, emotionally, and spiritually.

Silence the voice of fear. Break the grip of affliction. Let hope rise again in my heart. I receive Your peace and open my life to Your restoring touch. Thank You for loving me in the midst of my weakness. I wait for You, Healer of my soul. In Jesus' name, Amen.

DAY 2

When You Feel Anxious or Overwhelmed

The Circumstance

You're holding it together on the outside, but on the inside, it's unraveling. Your thoughts won't slow down. Your chest feels tight. The weight of responsibility, uncertainty, or fear presses in with no relief. You may not even know what triggered it—only that peace feels far away.

Encouragement

God is not overwhelmed by what overwhelms you. He is not surprised by your fear or frustrated by your anxiety. He meets you right in the middle of it. Even when you don't feel strong, you are not alone. He offers more than escape—He offers His presence, which is your peace.

Devotional Reflection

Anxiety can be loud. It spins worst-case scenarios, drowns out clarity, and steals rest. But Scripture offers an answer that seems almost too simple: *"Be still and know that I am God."* (Psalm 46:10) This isn't a command to ignore your fears but an invitation to remember who's greater than them.

In Philippians 4, Paul tells us to bring our anxiety to God with thanksgiving. Why? Because thanksgiving anchors us in truth. It shifts our focus from what we can't control to the One who holds all things together. And in that space—where we hand Him our worry—**His peace guards our hearts and minds**.

Peace doesn't always come from everything changing—it often comes when we realize that **God is with us even if nothing else changes yet**.

Let His peace speak louder than the panic.

Scripture

"Cast all your anxiety on Him because He cares for you."
— **1 Peter 5:7**

"Do not be anxious about anything, but in every situation, by prayer and petition, with thanksgiving, present your requests to God. And the peace of God... will guard your hearts and your minds in Christ Jesus."
— **Philippians 4:6–7**

"When my heart is overwhelmed, lead me to the rock that is higher than I."
— **Psalm 61:2**

Prayer

Lord, I feel overwhelmed. My thoughts are tangled, my heart is heavy, and peace feels distant. But right now, I choose to come to You—not with perfect words, but with open hands. I cast my anxiety on You. I release what I can't control. I breathe deep and ask You to still the storm within me.

Guard my heart and mind with Your peace. Speak truth to the lies that stir panic. Be the rock higher than my emotions. Thank You for loving me, calming me, and never leaving me alone in the storm. I rest in You. In Jesus' name, Amen.

DAY 3

When You're Waiting on God

The Circumstance

The waiting room of life can feel like the loneliest place in the world. You've prayed, believed, fasted, cried—and still, the answer hasn't come. The door remains closed. The silence is deafening. And while others seem to be moving forward, you feel stuck in pause. The ache of delay grows heavier each day.

Encouragement

Waiting is not wasting. In God's hands, waiting is working. Every moment you spend in delay, He's refining your faith, stretching your trust, and preparing you for the promise. God is never late. His timing is perfect. If He hasn't moved yet, it's not because He's forgotten you—it's because He's still weaving purpose into the answer.

Devotional Reflection

There are seasons when God seems silent—not absent, but quiet. In those seasons, we learn to lean not on outcomes but on His presence. Waiting teaches us to worship without answers, to trust without evidence, and to hope against all odds.

Think of Joseph—betrayed, falsely imprisoned, forgotten. Years passed between the promise and the promotion. But when the time came, no man could stop what God had set in motion. The waiting had prepared him to lead with wisdom, humility, and grace.

Your delay is not a denial. God is not punishing you with silence; He is forming something eternal within you. Strength. Endurance. Depth. Surrender.

So today, even if the breakthrough hasn't come—**praise Him anyway**. That praise is the seed of your harvest.

Scripture

"But those who wait on the Lord shall renew their strength; they shall mount up with wings like eagles, they shall run and not be weary, they shall walk and not faint."
— **Isaiah 40:31**

"The Lord is good to those who wait for Him, to the soul who seeks Him."
— **Lamentations 3:25**

"I wait for the Lord, my whole being waits, and in His word I put my hope."
— **Psalm 130:5**

Prayer

Father, waiting is hard. My heart is tired, and hope feels fragile. But I choose to believe that You are still at work—even in the silence. I surrender my timeline, my expectations, and my desire to control the outcome. I trust that You are preparing something good, something holy, something right.

Renew my strength as I wait. Give me grace to worship in the in-between. Teach me to anchor my hope in Your Word, not in my circumstances. And when the time is right, open the door no man can shut. Until then, I will wait with faith. In Jesus' name, Amen.

DAY 4

When All Your Plans Fall Apart

The Circumstance

You mapped it out. You prayed about it. You even felt peace moving forward. But now the plan is in pieces. The job didn't work out. The relationship ended. The opportunity fell through. What you thought would move you forward has left you questioning everything. You're left wondering, *Did I miss God? Was I wrong to hope?*

Encouragement

God is not confined to your plans—He's committed to your purpose. What falls apart in your hands may be falling into place in His. He is not a God of wasted seasons or pointless pain. When your plans collapse, His sovereignty remains. He knows what you don't. And He is still writing your story.

Devotional Reflection

When plans fall apart, it shakes more than our sense of direction—it often shakes our identity, our faith, and our confidence in hearing God. But Scripture shows us that even faithful people experienced devastating interruptions: Moses was sent to deliver Israel but was rejected at first. Paul was blocked from preaching in Asia and redirected to Macedonia. Even Jesus' followers didn't understand the cross until after the resurrection.

God allows some things to fall apart so He can build something better—something rooted not in our strength, but in His unshakable will. If it had worked the way you planned, you may have missed what He prepared.

So let the ashes testify that your God still rebuilds.

Scripture

"Many are the plans in a person's heart, but it is the Lord's purpose that prevails."
— Proverbs 19:21

"And we know that in all things God works for the good of those who love Him, who have been called according to His purpose."
— Romans 8:28

"Though He brings grief, He will show compassion, so great is His unfailing love. For He does not willingly bring affliction or grief to anyone."
— Lamentations 3:32–33

Prayer

God, I don't understand why things turned out this way. I followed You the best I knew how, but now I feel lost. Help me release the plan I thought would work and trust that You are still leading me.

I lay down my disappointment and pick up Your peace. Redirect my steps. Remind me that You are not finished. Where I see ruins, You see restoration. Thank You for loving me even when I'm confused and crushed. I trust Your heart when I can't see Your hand. In Jesus' name, Amen.

DAY 5

When You're Facing Financial Hardship

The Circumstance

The bills are piling up, the bank account is shrinking, and the weight of financial strain sits heavy on your chest. You're doing all you can—working, budgeting, praying—and still, it feels like there's never quite enough. Worry creeps in with every unexpected expense. Fear whispers questions: *Will I lose everything? How will I make it through this month?* And worst of all, you start to wonder, *Has God forgotten me?*

Encouragement

God sees your need before you even ask. He is Jehovah Jireh, the Lord who provides—not just barely, but faithfully, personally, and often miraculously. His provision is not always predictable, but it is always sufficient. You are not abandoned. He is working behind the scenes, even when the numbers don't add up.

Devotional Reflection

Financial hardship is more than a money issue—it touches your identity, your security, and your sense of stability. The enemy wants you to believe that lack means failure or that need equals abandonment. But God often does His deepest work in seasons of dependence. In the wilderness, He fed Israel with manna from heaven—just enough for each day. They couldn't store it up or predict it. They simply had to trust.

Jesus taught us to pray, *"Give us this day our daily bread."* That prayer isn't just about food—it's about daily dependence. God often allows tight seasons not to punish us, but to teach us how to walk by faith and not by sight. Sometimes He opens a door. Sometimes He sends help through others. And sometimes, He strengthens your faith in the waiting.

Provision will come. Peace will come. And when it does, you'll know without a doubt—it was God who sustained you.

Scripture

"And my God will supply every need of yours according to His riches in glory in Christ Jesus."
— **Philippians 4:19**

"The lions may grow weak and hungry, but those who seek the Lord lack no good thing."
— **Psalm 34:10**

"So do not worry, saying, 'What shall we eat?' or 'What shall we drink?' or 'What shall we wear?'... Your heavenly Father knows that you need them."
— **Matthew 6:31–32**

Prayer

Lord, I feel the pressure of financial need, and it's weighing on my heart. I confess the fear, the frustration, and the helplessness that come when ends don't meet. But today, I shift my eyes from the need to the Source. You are my Provider. You own the cattle on a thousand hills. You see what I lack, and You are not limited by earthly resources.

Teach me to trust You daily. Open the doors I cannot open. Stretch what I have. Provide in ways I can't yet see. And through it all, remind me that I am loved, not forgotten. I trust You to sustain me. In Jesus' name, Amen.

DAY 6

When You've Been Waiting a Long Time and the Answer Hasn't Come

The Circumstance

You believed. You prayed. You've stood in faith longer than most people know. But the answer still hasn't come. Days turned into months. Months into years. People moved on. Seasons changed. And yet you're still waiting—still hoping, still asking, still hurting. Somewhere deep inside, the question whispers: *Has God changed His mind... or has He changed His mind about me?*

Encouragement

God has not forgotten you. Delay is not denial. The length of the wait doesn't diminish the power of the promise. God's silence is not absence, and His timing isn't punishment—it's preparation. What feels like a delay is often grace, holding back the answer until you're ready, until the ground is ready, until the miracle can do its full work.

Devotional Reflection

Long waits are some of the hardest tests of faith. You're not just waiting for a thing—you're waiting with a heart that aches, with prayers that feel unanswered, with hope that gets bruised each time the door doesn't open.

Abraham waited 25 years for Isaac. David was anointed king but returned to the sheepfold for years. Hannah waited in sorrow and silence before her womb was opened. And still, God was faithful. Why? Because what He was doing in them during the wait was just as important as what He would do through them after it.

In the waiting, your faith is purified. Your motives are refined. Your strength is tested. And you discover that your hope is not just in the outcome—it's in the One who holds the outcome.

He hasn't forgotten. He's still working. And when the answer comes, it will be more beautiful than anything you could have orchestrated on your own.

Scripture

"Hope deferred makes the heart sick, but a longing fulfilled is a tree of life."
— Proverbs 13:12

"Let us not become weary in doing good, for at the proper time we will reap a harvest if we do not give up."
— Galatians 6:9

"The Lord is not slow in keeping His promise, as some understand slowness. Instead, He is patient..."
— 2 Peter 3:9

Prayer

Lord, I don't understand the delay. I'm tired of waiting. My heart is stretched thin, and hope feels fragile. But I will not give up. I believe You still hear me. I believe You are still working, even in the silence. I lay down the timelines I created and receive Your timing instead.

Strengthen me in the wait. Anchor me in Your promises. Heal the discouragement that has crept into my soul. Help me trust not just what You do—but who You are. I know You are good, and I believe Your goodness is still coming for me. In Jesus' name, Amen.

DAY 7

When You Feel Alone or Forgotten

The Circumstance

You smile in public, but deep down you feel invisible. People come and go, conversations move around you, and yet it feels like no one truly sees you—no one checks in, no one notices the weight you carry. Prayers feel like they're hitting a closed ceiling, and the silence of God feels heavier than the silence of people. In your heart, the ache asks: *Does anyone see me? Has even God forgotten me?*

Encouragement

You are not alone, and you have not been forgotten. God sees you—every sigh, every tear, every unspoken word. His eyes never left you, even when others did. You are not abandoned; you are held in the palm of His hand. Heaven has not gone silent. He is closer than your next breath, even when your heart feels isolated.

Devotional Reflection

One of the deepest human needs is to be seen, known, and loved. When that need is unmet, especially in hard seasons, it can lead to despair. But Scripture shows us that many of God's greatest servants felt this same ache—Elijah, after calling down fire, sat under a tree and begged to die, feeling utterly alone. Hagar, cast out and forgotten in the desert, wept by a spring—and there, God met her.

He didn't send an army or a miracle first—He called her by name and gave her a new name for Him: *El Roi*—"the God who sees me."

You serve that same God. He sees the unseen. He listens to the unheard. And He doesn't just observe—He moves with compassion. He may not fill the room with people right away, but He will always fill your soul with His presence.

You are seen. You are loved. You are remembered.

Scripture

*"Can a woman forget her nursing child, and not have compassion on the son of her womb? Surely they may forget, yet I will not forget you. See, I have inscribed you on the **palms of My** hands..."*
— **Isaiah 49:15–16**

"The Lord is close to the brokenhearted and saves those who are crushed in spirit."
— **Psalm 34:18**

"You see me, Lord. You know me."
— **Jeremiah 12:3a**

Prayer

God, I feel forgotten. I feel unseen in this world and unheard in my prayers. But today, I reach for You—not for answers, but for Your presence. Remind me that You have never left. Let Your nearness soothe the ache in my soul. Whisper to my heart that I am not alone.

You are El Roi—the God who sees me. You see beyond my performance and my pain. You know my story, and You call me by name. Fill the empty spaces with Your peace. And help me believe again that I matter —not just to people, but to You. In Jesus' name, Amen.

DAY 8

When You're Grieving a Loss

The Circumstance

Something—or someone—you loved is gone, and the absence is deafening. Grief is a weight you didn't choose but now carry daily. People may expect you to move on, but every room, memory, and routine reminds you of what's no longer there. You wonder if the ache will ever ease or if the tears will ever stop. Even joy feels out of reach. And sometimes, so does God.

Encouragement

Grief is not weakness—it's love with nowhere to go. It's a sacred ache that honors what mattered deeply. And in your sorrow, God does not step back—He draws closer. He doesn't rush your healing or silence your pain. Instead, He sits with you in the dark and reminds you that you are not alone. Your tears are seen. Your sorrow is safe with Him.

Devotional Reflection

Jesus wept. The shortest verse in the Bible carries eternal comfort. Standing before Lazarus' tomb, knowing He would raise him from the dead, Jesus still wept—because grief is holy ground, and God never rushes through our pain.

There is a time to mourn. And mourning is not the absence of faith—it is the expression of it. You mourn because you loved. And

God, who is love, understands.

Psalm 56 says He keeps every tear in a bottle—not one is lost or unnoticed. Heaven does not ignore your sorrow. And while grief may never fully leave, God promises to walk with you through it, comforting, restoring, and slowly helping you breathe again.

In time, He will trade your ashes for beauty, your mourning for joy. Not by erasing what was lost—but by healing the wound it left behind.

Scripture

"The Lord is close to the brokenhearted and saves those who are crushed in spirit."
— Psalm 34:18

"Blessed are those who mourn, for they will be comforted."
— Matthew 5:4

"You keep track of all my sorrows. You have collected all my tears in your bottle."
— Psalm 56:8 (NLT)

Prayer

God, this loss hurts more than words can say. I miss what was. I ache for what will never be again. I don't know how to move forward, but I know I don't want to walk this road without You. Be near to me in my grief. Hold my heart in its brokenness. Remind me that You are not afraid of sorrow, and You do not rush healing.

Comfort me in ways no person can. Help me honor what I've lost while holding onto what remains. Give me strength for today and hope for tomorrow. And when the tears come, let them fall into Your hands. In Jesus' name, Amen.

DAY 9

When A Friend Betrays You

The Circumstance

They were supposed to be safe. You trusted them. You shared your heart, your secrets, your journey—and then something shifted. Maybe it was subtle, maybe it was sudden. But now you're left with the sting of betrayal: the silence, the slander, the abandonment. What once felt like a blessing now feels like a wound. And you're left with questions like: *How could they do this? Did I mean so little to them?*

Encouragement

Betrayal is one of the deepest human wounds—because it comes not from enemies, but from those once close. But even here, you are not alone. Jesus understands this pain intimately. He was betrayed by one of His own, with a kiss no less. And yet—even in that moment—He chose love, truth, and surrender. He did not let the betrayal define Him, and neither will you.

Devotional Reflection

When someone close betrays us, it can distort the way we view people, relationships, and even God. The enemy uses betrayal to plant bitterness. But God uses it to reveal what's unshakable.

Jesus didn't retaliate when Judas handed Him over. Instead, He grieved the betrayal, but He also trusted the Father's plan. That doesn't make betrayal less painful—but it does give us a path forward: to feel the pain without becoming the pain.

Forgiveness doesn't excuse what happened. It releases your soul from being bound to it. Healing doesn't mean pretending it didn't matter. It means surrendering the justice to the One who sees all and repays with righteousness.

God will heal what was broken, restore what was lost, and bring new, healthy connections in time. But even before that happens—He will restore your peace.

Scripture

"Even my close friend, someone I trusted, one who shared my bread, has turned against me."
— Psalm 41:9

"Jesus said, 'Friend, do what you came for.' Then the men stepped forward, seized Jesus and arrested Him."
— Matthew 26:50

"The Lord is faithful, and He will strengthen you and protect you from the evil one."
— 2 Thessalonians 3:3

Prayer

Lord, betrayal cuts deep. I trusted someone who hurt me, and my heart is struggling to make sense of it. Help me release the bitterness before it takes root. Help me forgive—not because they deserve it, but because I need freedom. You were betrayed too, and You didn't let it stop Your purpose. Help me walk in that same strength.

Heal the wounded places. Protect my heart from becoming hard. And show me that You are still the Friend who sticks closer than a brother. Thank You for never turning on me. In Jesus' name, Amen.

DAY 10

When You Feel Unworthy or Ashamed

The Circumstance

You can't shake the voice in your head: *You're not good enough. You'll never be enough. Look at what you've done.* Whether it's a past mistake, a hidden struggle, or a deeply rooted insecurity, shame has wrapped itself around your heart. You find yourself disqualifying your own prayers, doubting your value, and wondering how God could still want you.

Encouragement

Shame is a liar, but grace tells the truth. And the truth is this: you are still loved, still chosen, still redeemable. Jesus did not die for the version of you that has it all together. He died for the real you —the one with wounds, regrets, and mess. Grace doesn't excuse sin; it covers it, cleanses it, and calls you forward.

Devotional Reflection

The enemy uses shame to silence you, isolate you, and paralyze your purpose. But the cross silences shame. When Jesus died, He carried not only your sin—but your guilt and your humiliation. Hebrews 12:2 says He endured the cross, *"despising the shame."* He scorned it. He disarmed it. He broke its power.

God is not repelled by your weakness—He is drawn to it. That's where His strength shines brightest. When the prodigal son returned home in shame, the father ran to him—not with rebuke, but with a robe. That's how the Father sees you. He knows everything, and He still wants you.

You don't have to earn your way back. You only have to come.

Scripture

"There is therefore now no condemnation for those who are in Christ Jesus."
— Romans 8:1

"Those who look to Him are radiant; their faces are never covered with shame."
— Psalm 34:5

"As far as the east is from the west, so far has He removed our transgressions from us."
— Psalm 103:12

Prayer

Father, I feel unworthy. Shame clings to me like a shadow. But today I choose to believe what You say over what I feel. You call me clean. You call me loved. You call me Yours. Wash over me with Your mercy. Break the lies that keep me stuck. Help me see myself the way You see me— not through the lens of failure, but through the lens of the cross.

I lay down my guilt. I step into Your grace. I receive Your embrace. Thank You that nothing I've done can outrun the blood of Jesus. In His name I pray, Amen.

DAY 11

When You're Battling Depression

The Circumstance

The heaviness doesn't lift. You wake up tired, carry sadness without cause, and feel like joy is locked behind glass you can't break. Even the simplest tasks feel overwhelming. People may not understand, and you may not even understand yourself. You love God, but the darkness feels unrelenting. You wonder: *Where is my breakthrough? Will I ever feel light again?*

Encouragement

Depression is not a failure of faith. It's not a punishment or a sign of weakness. Even the strongest saints have faced the depths of despair. But you are not alone—not in your thoughts, not in your silence, and not in your sadness. Jesus is with you in the dark, and He doesn't flinch at your pain. He holds your hand, not your performance.

Devotional Reflection

David wrote psalms in the cave. Elijah asked God to take his life. Jeremiah wept for chapters. Depression is not new to God, and it does not scare Him. He does not shame you for it—He walks with you through it.

God's healing may come through Scripture, through supernatural peace, or through the wisdom of counseling and treatment. There is no shame in seeking help. Sometimes, healing is both spiritual and practical, and God uses both prayer and people to bring relief.

But in the meantime, cling to this: your feelings are not the truth —God's Word is. And His Word says you are loved, not forsaken; chosen, not condemned; held, not hopeless. You may not feel light now, but light is coming. And until it fully breaks, the Light of the world walks with you.

Scripture

"Why, my soul, are you downcast? Why so disturbed within me? Put your hope in God, for I will yet praise Him…"
— Psalm 42:11

"The light shines in the darkness, and the darkness has not overcome it."
— John 1:5

"Even though I walk through the darkest valley, I will fear no evil, for You are with me…"
— Psalm 23:4

Prayer

Lord, I'm tired of pretending to be okay. I'm worn out by the weight I carry. I ask You to meet me here—in the dark, in the silence, in the sadness. I don't ask for a quick fix. I ask for Your presence. Be my strength when I have none. Be my light when I can't see. Be my comfort when nothing else reaches the ache.

Remind me that I'm not weak for feeling this way. And show me, moment by moment, that I'm not alone. Help me take each step with You, even when I don't feel it. I trust You to bring beauty from this place. In Jesus' name, Amen.

DAY 12

When You Need Direction

The Circumstance

You've prayed, waited, and sought counsel—but you're still unsure which way to go. There's more than one option, and none feel clear. Or maybe the path ahead feels foggy, with no obvious next step. You don't want to make the wrong move, but standing still feels like stagnation. Inside, you're crying out: *God, what do You want me to do?*

Encouragement

God is not playing hide-and-seek with His will. He is a faithful Shepherd who promises to lead you—not just when the road is obvious, but especially when it's not. You don't have to fear missing His direction when your heart is surrendered to His voice. He will guide you step by step, even if you can't see the whole map right now.

Devotional Reflection

Sometimes we think God only speaks through burning bushes and parted seas—but most often, He leads through peace, through His Word, and through steady nudges in our spirit. The book of Proverbs says, *"In all your ways acknowledge Him, and He will direct your path."* That means God responds not just to your prayers, but to your daily dependence.

When we seek His will more than our own comfort, He honors that. When we lay down our fear of failure and pick up trust, He meets us there. The goal is not just to arrive at the "right place," but to walk with the right Person every step of the way.

If you don't know what to do yet, it's okay to wait. Clarity often comes after surrender. And remember: sometimes God's "no" or "not yet" is the most loving direction of all.

Scripture

"Trust in the Lord with all your heart and lean not on your own understanding; in all your ways submit to Him, and He will make your paths straight."
— **Proverbs 3:5–6**

"Whether you turn to the right or to the left, your ears will hear a voice behind you, saying, 'This is the way; walk in it.'"
— **Isaiah 30:21**

"The steps of a good man are ordered by the Lord: and He delighteth in his way."
— **Psalm 37:23 (KJV)**

Prayer

Lord, I need Your direction. I don't want to lean on my own understanding or be paralyzed by fear of getting it wrong. Help me to trust that You are guiding me—even when I can't see the full picture. Quiet the noise. Clear the confusion. Give me wisdom, and lead me with Your peace.

If You say wait, help me to wait with grace. If You say go, help me to walk in confidence. I surrender my plans and ask for Your purpose. Thank You for being the Shepherd of my path. In Jesus' name, Amen.

DAY 13

When God's Will Is Not What You Want

The Circumstance

You prayed with passion. You believed with faith. You hoped with everything you had. But the outcome you desperately wanted didn't happen. The door closed. The relationship ended. The healing didn't come. And now you're sitting with the tension of wanting to trust God—but also feeling disappointed by what He allowed.

Encouragement

God's will isn't always easy—but it is always good, wise, and perfect. Even when it breaks your heart, it does not break His love for you. He sees the whole picture. And though He may not give you what you wanted, He will never withhold what you truly need to become who He created you to be.

Devotional Reflection

Surrender is one of the hardest parts of faith—especially when God's will contradicts your deepest desires. Jesus Himself wrestled in Gethsemane, praying, *"If it be possible, let this cup pass from Me."* But then He said the words that changed everything: *"Nevertheless, not My will, but Yours be done."*

It's okay to be honest with God about your disappointment. He invites your tears. But what He asks for in return is your trust

—not because He needs control, but because He longs to protect, mature, and bless you through the path only He can see.

Faith is not just believing when things go your way. It's believing when they don't, and trusting that God is still for you. That He still knows what He's doing. That what feels like a loss may one day prove to be a divine rescue.

The cross didn't look like victory either—until three days later.

Scripture

"Father, if You are willing, take this cup from Me; yet not My will, but Yours be done."
— **Luke 22:42**

"As for God, His way is perfect: The Lord's word is flawless; He shields all who take refuge in Him."
— **Psalm 18:30**

"And we know that in all things God works for the good of those who love Him..."
— **Romans 8:28**

Prayer

Father, I don't understand. I don't like this outcome. I trusted You, and this wasn't what I hoped for. But I still choose You. I surrender my will —not out of defeat, but out of trust. Help me lay down my desires and pick up faith.

Even when I don't get what I want, let me never doubt who You are. You are good. You are God. And I am still in Your hands. In Jesus' name, Amen.

DAY 14

When You Have Irreconcilable Differences With a Family Member

The Circumstance

You love them—but the relationship is strained, complicated, or completely broken. Every conversation ends in conflict, or maybe silence has taken over. No matter how hard you try, you can't seem to get through. The gap feels unbridgeable. You've prayed. You've apologized. You've forgiven. But reconciliation feels impossible, and it hurts more than words can express.

Encouragement

Family pain cuts deep—but God understands fractured relationships. He sees your efforts and your heart. Reconciliation takes two, but healing can begin with one. Even if peace with them isn't possible right now, peace within you is still God's promise. He will heal the ache, guide your boundaries, and keep you anchored in grace.

Devotional Reflection

God's Word calls us to seek peace and pursue it, but it also acknowledges the reality that not all peace is possible in this life. Romans 12:18 reminds us, *"If it is possible, as far as it depends on you, live at peace with everyone."* That "if" matters. It means that sometimes, despite your best efforts, peace may not come.

When family relationships are broken, it doesn't mean you're a failure. It means you're human. Jesus Himself experienced rejection from His own hometown and was misunderstood by His earthly family. And still, He walked in love, grace, and truth.

You can forgive without reopening toxic patterns. You can honor someone from a distance. You can grieve what's been lost while still walking in freedom.

God is not asking you to carry what's not yours. He's asking you to release it into His hands and trust that He is the only One who sees every motive, every wound, and every hidden place.

Scripture

"If it is possible, as far as it depends on you, live at peace with everyone."
— Romans 12:18

"Turn from evil and do good; seek peace and pursue it."
— Psalm 34:14

"Make every effort to live in peace with everyone and to be holy; without holiness no one will see the Lord."
— Hebrews 12:14

Prayer

God, this relationship hurts. I've tried to make it right, but the distance remains. Help me not to carry guilt for what I can't control. Show me how to love well—whether that means reaching out or stepping back. Give me discernment to know when to speak and when to stay silent.

Heal my heart from the pain of misunderstanding, rejection, and disappointment. I release them to You, and I choose forgiveness again today. Even if restoration never comes, let restoration come within me. I trust You to be the peacekeeper when I can't be. In Jesus' name, Amen.

DAY 15

When Your Adult Children Have Rejected You

The Circumstance

You carried them, nurtured them, sacrificed for them. You gave your best, even when it wasn't perfect. But now, the relationship is fractured—or completely cut off. Your calls go unanswered. Your name is left out. You hear about their lives from others, or not at all. And worse still, your love is misinterpreted, your sacrifices forgotten. You wonder, *What did I do wrong? Why won't they let me love them anymore?*

Encouragement

God sees your tears. He understands the ache of rejected love. He, too, is a Father who has been turned away by His own children. You are not alone in this pain. Your heartbreak is sacred to Him. You may not be able to change their hearts, but you can entrust them to the One who never stops pursuing prodigals—even when they're grown.

Devotional Reflection

Parental love is one of the most God-like kinds of love: it gives, sacrifices, hopes, corrects, and forgives. And when that love is rejected, the wound reaches deeper than words can express.

But remember this: God is not holding you hostage to their decisions. Your identity is not dependent on their approval, their gratitude, or their return. You are still a parent, still worthy of honor, still wrapped in the love of your Heavenly Father.

Like the father in Luke 15, you may be watching the road, praying through the pain. But just as that story shows, God specializes in homecomings. Even if they're still far off, He can reach them. In the meantime, don't stop loving—but also don't lose yourself trying to fix what only He can heal.

Your prayers are seeds. Your love is not wasted. Your pain is not unseen.

Scripture

"Train up a child in the way he should go, and when he is old, he will not depart from it."
— Proverbs 22:6

"The Lord is close to the brokenhearted and saves those who are crushed in spirit."
— Psalm 34:18

"He will turn the hearts of the parents to their children, and the hearts of the children to their parents…"
— Malachi 4:6a

Prayer

Father, my heart is breaking. I never imagined that love could be rejected like this. You know what it is to be forsaken by Your own, and You know the pain of longing for a child to return. So I bring this sorrow to You. I lift up my child and release them into Your care.

Heal what I cannot reach. Speak what I cannot say. And protect my heart from growing bitter or numb. Remind me that You are still writing the story. Comfort me when the silence is loud. And give me hope for restoration—even if I can't see how. I entrust my child to You, the Perfect Parent. In Jesus' name, Amen.

DAY 16

When an Elderly Parent Is Facing Dementia

The Circumstance

They were once strong, sharp, and full of wisdom. Now, you watch them slip away—moment by moment, memory by memory. Their words don't always make sense. Their personality shifts. Some days they recognize you. Other days they don't. You grieve not a sudden loss, but a slow, daily unraveling. You're caught between caregiving and mourning, between honoring who they were and coping with who they're becoming.

Encouragement

God sees both of you—your parent in their fading dignity, and you in your faithful love. He is present in every forgotten name, every repeated story, every heavy sigh. Dementia may steal memory, but it cannot erase identity in Christ. Your parent is still known by God, even when they no longer know themselves. And you are not unseen in your care.

Devotional Reflection

It's hard to watch someone you love disappear in front of you. It feels like a betrayal of time—a slow undoing of all that was precious and familiar. But even in this, God remains. He is the Keeper of our minds and the Guardian of our hearts. His Spirit is not limited by brain chemistry or cognitive clarity.

The Bible honors those who care for aging parents, not just in word but in spirit. Jesus Himself, even while hanging on the cross, ensured His mother would be cared for. That's how seriously God regards what you're doing.

You don't have to carry the weight alone. Invite God into the routine, the breakdowns, the guilt, the exhaustion, and even the anger. He will give you grace for each moment, and compassion when yours runs dry.

There is still beauty in this chapter. And though their memory may fade, your love leaves a lasting mark that dementia can never touch.

Scripture

"Even to your old age and gray hairs I am He, I am He who will sustain you. I have made you and I will carry you; I will sustain you and I will rescue you."
— Isaiah 46:4

"Honor your father and your mother…"
— Exodus 20:12

"Do not cast me away when I am old; do not forsake me when my strength is gone."
— Psalm 71:9

Prayer

Lord, this journey is painful and exhausting. I miss who my parent used to be, and I'm grieving the slow loss. Give me strength to keep showing up. Give me compassion when I feel numb. Give me grace when I run out of patience. Help me see Your face in theirs, even when they forget mine.

Sustain me in the caregiving. Speak peace into my sadness. Let Your Spirit rest in our home. And hold my parent close, especially when their mind drifts far away. I trust that You remember what they've forgotten. And You will never forget me either. In Jesus' name, Amen.

DAY 17

When Your Family Is Broken

The Circumstance

There's tension, silence, distance—or worse, open conflict. Words have been said that can't be unsaid. Maybe it's been years of dysfunction, or maybe something shattered suddenly. Holidays feel heavy. Group texts are quiet. Love still lingers, but it's buried beneath pain. You ask yourself, *How did we get here? And will we ever be whole again?*

Encouragement

Family is God's design—but even in Scripture, families were messy and broken. God does some of His most redemptive work in the midst of family pain. He sees what's fractured, and He knows how to restore what feels impossible. Your cries are heard, your pain is known, and your faithfulness matters—even when you're the only one fighting for peace.

Devotional Reflection

Abraham lied. Jacob deceived. Joseph was betrayed by his brothers. David's family was torn by violence and grief. Even Jesus' own family misunderstood Him. The Bible doesn't hide the reality of broken homes—it reveals a God who steps right into them and begins healing.

You may not be able to fix every fracture, and reconciliation may not come overnight—or ever in some cases. But that doesn't mean healing can't begin. It starts in you. It starts with prayer, humility, and surrender. It starts with letting go of blame and bitterness, even when you still carry the scars.

You are not responsible for everyone's choices, but you are accountable for how you respond. And even if the family never looks like it used to, God can bring beauty into the brokenness and restore joy into the ruins.

He is the God who makes all things new—even families.

Scripture

"He heals the brokenhearted and binds up their wounds."
— Psalm 147:3

"The Lord is close to the brokenhearted and saves those who are crushed in spirit."
— Psalm 34:18

"I will restore to you the years that the swarming locust has eaten…"
— Joel 2:25a

Prayer

Lord, my heart aches over my family. What once felt safe and whole now feels scattered and painful. I confess the bitterness, the exhaustion, the disappointment. And I invite You into the mess. Heal what I can't. Speak where silence has grown loud. Bring understanding where there's been confusion.

Help me love even when it hurts. Help me forgive even when it's undeserved. And remind me that You are still able to restore what's broken—whether in part or in full. Make me an instrument of peace in my family. In Jesus' name, Amen.

DAY 18

When You're Struggling in Marriage

The Circumstance

The connection feels distant. The conversations are strained—or absent. What used to be filled with love and unity now feels like a battlefield or a cold silence. You're trying to hold on, but disappointment, unmet needs, or repeated hurt are taking their toll. You wonder, *Is restoration even possible? Or have we just grown too far apart?*

Encouragement

Marriage is not easy, even for people who love God. But it is holy ground—a covenant God cares deeply about. He sees what you're carrying, and He knows both of your hearts. While you cannot force change, you can fight in the Spirit—for healing, for softness, for connection. God is still able to breathe life into dry places.

Devotional Reflection

Struggles in marriage can be some of the most isolating and painful battles. Because it's not just the loss of affection—it's the ache of broken intimacy, of dreams fading, of trust tested. Yet throughout Scripture, God consistently uses marriage as a picture of His love: faithful, enduring, sacrificial.

Love is not sustained by emotion alone. It's fueled by surrender, humility, forgiveness, and a willingness to stay even when leaving feels easier. That doesn't mean tolerating abuse or betrayal without boundaries—it means pursuing God's heart and asking Him to show you how to love in truth and strength.

Sometimes He revives marriages. Sometimes He transforms hearts one layer at a time. Sometimes He gives supernatural wisdom to know how to respond. But in every case, He walks with you through it. He is not a distant observer—He is the Restorer.

Don't give up on what God has joined without first inviting Him fully into the center.

Scripture

"Though one may be overpowered, two can defend themselves. A cord of three strands is not quickly broken."
— Ecclesiastes 4:12

"Above all, love each other deeply, because love covers over a multitude of sins."
— 1 Peter 4:8

"Be completely humble and gentle; be patient, bearing with one another in love."
— Ephesians 4:2

Prayer

Lord, You see the struggle in my marriage. You know the words we don't say, the tension we carry, and the things we've lost along the way. I bring it all to You—every hurt, every fear, every hope. Soften our hearts. Remind us who we were when love began. Show us how to fight for each other, not against each other.

Where we've grown apart, build a bridge. Where trust has broken, rebuild it with grace. And where love has dimmed, ignite it again through Your Spirit. Teach me to love like You do—sacrificially, patiently, and wisely. In Jesus' name, Amen.

DAY 19

When You Must Deal With a Cheating Spouse

The Circumstance

You never imagined this would happen. The one who vowed to love you has broken that vow. Trust has shattered. The foundation of your covenant feels cracked beyond repair. You're filled with questions: *Was it me? Can I ever trust again? Should I stay?* The betrayal is more than physical—it's emotional, spiritual, and deeply personal. And no one really knows the weight you're carrying.

Encouragement

God sees the secret agony. He hears the silent sobs. He does not take betrayal lightly—and neither should you. But while people may offer shame, revenge, or confusion, God offers clarity, compassion, and healing. He won't force your decision—but He will walk with you no matter what you choose. You are not alone. You are not at fault for someone else's sin. And you are not without hope.

Devotional Reflection

Adultery is one of the deepest relational wounds because it strikes at the core of covenant. It was never God's will for your heart to be torn like this. And if you're angry, devastated, or numb—you are not weak. You are human. Even God, in Scripture, describes the pain of Israel's unfaithfulness as spiritual adultery, and His response is one of righteous grief.

Now is not the time for hasty decisions or rushed emotions. It's the time to lean hard into God—for wisdom, for boundaries, for peace in the chaos. Some marriages recover after adultery. Some do not. But what matters first is your healing.

God is your Defender, your Counselor, and your Comforter. He will not lead you into bitterness or bondage. He will give you clarity where there is confusion. He will protect your dignity, even when others try to diminish it. And if you choose to fight for the marriage, He will walk with you. If you must release it, He will catch every piece of your heart.

Scripture

"The Lord is close to the brokenhearted and saves those who are crushed in spirit."
— Psalm 34:18

"You keep him in perfect peace whose mind is stayed on You, because he trusts in You."
— Isaiah 26:3

"The Lord will fight for you; you need only to be still."
— Exodus 14:14

Prayer

God, my heart is broken and my trust is shattered. I never thought I'd be here, facing betrayal from the one I loved. I need You now more than ever. Speak truth where lies have invaded. Speak peace where fear has taken over. Give me wisdom for what to do next. Surround me with godly counsel, not judgment.

Heal the wounds I can't explain. Restore what the enemy has tried to steal from my soul. I refuse to carry shame that doesn't belong to me. I rest in Your love. I wait for Your clarity. I lean into Your arms. Whether You lead me to fight or to walk away, I know You will never leave me. In

Jesus' name, Amen.

DAY 20

When You've Lost a Job or Opportunity

The Circumstance

You thought it was secure. You thought the door was open. Maybe it was a promotion you prepared for, a career you invested in, or an opportunity that felt tailor-made for your next season. But it slipped away—unexpectedly, unfairly, or through circumstances beyond your control. Now you're left with grief, confusion, and the quiet fear: *What now?*

Encouragement

God is not confined to one door, one employer, or one opportunity. He is your Source—not the job, not the title, not the position. When something ends, it's not the end of your calling. It may be the beginning of something greater, something only He could orchestrate in the unseen. He is still writing your story.

Devotional Reflection

Job loss or missed opportunities can rattle your sense of identity. So much of our confidence and security can unknowingly become tied to what we do. But in Christ, your worth is never defined by a paycheck or position—it's rooted in your unchanging identity as a child of God.

David was overlooked by his father and passed over by people before he was crowned king. Joseph was thrown into prison before he stood in Pharaoh's court. Paul's ministry was redirected multiple times. What looked like detours were really divine alignments.

God knows how to restore, reposition, and redeem. And while grief is valid, you don't have to stay in despair. What you lost does not compare to what God still has in store.

Scripture

"For I know the plans I have for you," declares the Lord, "plans to prosper you and not to harm you, plans to give you a hope and a future."
— Jeremiah 29:11

"And we know that in all things God works for the good of those who love Him, who have been called according to His purpose."
— Romans 8:28

"Weeping may endure for a night, but joy comes in the morning."
— Psalm 30:5b

Prayer

God, I didn't see this coming. I worked hard, prayed, believed—and now I feel lost. I bring You my disappointment, my frustration, and the fear of what's next. I ask You to steady my heart and restore my hope. Remind me that no door closes without Your permission—and no closed door can cancel Your plan.

Help me see beyond what I've lost and trust You for what's ahead. Open a new path. Provide where I lack. And strengthen my faith while I wait. Thank You that my identity is not in what I do, but in who I am in You. In Jesus' name, Amen.

DAY 21

When You're Facing Injustice

The Circumstance

You were wronged. Lied about. Overlooked. Judged unfairly. You did what was right, and still ended up hurt. Maybe others don't know, maybe they don't care—but you do. And the pain cuts deep, especially when you've honored God but received betrayal or silence in return. You want to forgive, but part of you also cries out: *Where is the justice?*

Encouragement

God is a righteous Judge, and He sees every injustice—even the ones done in secret. He is not blind to what happened or silent about what it cost you. His justice may not come on your timeline, but it will come in His perfect way. And while you wait, He defends your peace, your worth, and your integrity.

Devotional Reflection

Injustice is not just unfair—it's disorienting. It makes you question truth, question people, even question God. But Scripture is full of faithful people who faced injustice: Joseph was imprisoned for a lie. Daniel was thrown to lions for praying. Jesus Himself was tried unfairly, mocked, and crucified for doing no wrong.

God didn't abandon them—and He won't abandon you. What man

intends for harm, God is still able to use for good. That doesn't mean injustice becomes acceptable. It means it will not define your end.

You don't have to carry the burden of revenge. You don't have to force your own vindication. Your job is to remain faithful—His job is to make all things right. Keep standing. Keep trusting. And know this: He will not let your righteousness be forgotten.

Scripture

"For the Lord is a God of justice; blessed are all who wait for Him!"
— Isaiah 30:18

"Do not take revenge, my dear friends, but leave room for God's wrath, for it is written: 'It is mine to avenge; I will repay,' says the Lord."
— Romans 12:19

"He will make your righteous reward shine like the dawn, your vindication like the noonday sun."
— Psalm 37:6

Prayer

Lord, I've been treated unfairly, and my heart is heavy with the weight of injustice. I want to respond in truth and grace, but my flesh is tired and hurt. Help me release the need to be vindicated. Help me trust that You see what others don't.

Defend me, Lord. Heal me from the wounds of injustice. Protect my character, and let no bitterness take root. I choose to walk uprightly, even when I've been wronged. And I trust You to make all things right in Your time. In Jesus' name, Amen.

DAY 22

When You're Afraid of the Future

The Circumstance

The unknown looms ahead like a fog. You can't see the next step, let alone the full path. The world feels unstable, plans fall through, and everything in you wants to feel safe—but fear whispers worst-case scenarios. Your thoughts spiral: *What if I fail? What if I lose everything? What if God doesn't come through this time?*

Encouragement

The future is unknown to you, but it's already seen by God. He stands outside of time, holding both your now and your not-yet. Nothing about your future will ever surprise Him. You don't have to know what's coming to have peace. You only have to know who's already there.

Devotional Reflection

Fear thrives in uncertainty. It feeds off of imagined outcomes and false stories. But Scripture tells us to *"cast our cares upon the Lord,"* not because they're small, but because He cares for us deeply. He doesn't dismiss your fears—He carries them.

Jesus said, *"Do not worry about tomorrow,"* not as a rebuke, but as an invitation: *Trust Me with what you can't see.* The Israelites in the wilderness had no road map—just a cloud by day and fire by night. God led them one step at a time, and He'll do the same for you.

You don't need all the answers. You just need to walk with the One who is the Alpha and the Omega, the Beginning and the End. And if the future feels overwhelming, remember: grace doesn't come in advance—it comes right on time.

Scripture

"For I know the plans I have for you," declares the Lord, "plans to prosper you and not to harm you, plans to give you a hope and a future."
— **Jeremiah 29:11**

"When I am afraid, I put my trust in You."
— **Psalm 56:3**

"Therefore do not worry about tomorrow, for tomorrow will worry about itself."
— **Matthew 6:34**

Prayer

Lord, the future feels uncertain, and fear has crept into my heart. I'm trying to trust You, but the unknown makes me anxious. Help me let go of the illusion of control and rest in Your sovereignty. Calm the storm in my thoughts. Steady my faith. Remind me that You're already in my tomorrow, preparing the way.

I choose to believe that no matter what comes, You will be with me. And that is enough. I trust You with what I don't understand, and I surrender the future into Your loving hands. In Jesus' name, Amen.

DAY 23

When You Feel Spiritually Dry

The Circumstance

Your prayers feel empty. Your Bible sits closed. Worship doesn't stir your soul like it used to. You believe—but something inside feels numb, distant, dry. You're going through the motions, but the fire that once burned bright now feels like fading embers. And deep down, you wonder: *What's wrong with me? Has God pulled away?*

Encouragement

Dry seasons are not evidence of God's absence—they are often invitations into deeper trust. Even when you don't feel Him, He is still near. The God who once poured out rivers is still able to fill your well again. You are not forsaken. You are not failing. You are simply being drawn closer than emotion can carry you.

Devotional Reflection

Spiritual dryness can feel like wilderness—but remember, the wilderness is where God shaped His people. It's where He spoke to Moses, fed Israel, and prepared Jesus for ministry. It's not a place of punishment—it's a place of transformation.

David cried out, *"My soul thirsts for You in a dry and weary land..."* (Psalm 63:1). Even he, the man after God's own heart, felt empty at times. But he didn't stop seeking. He pressed in—not because he felt like it, but because he knew God was still worthy.

You may not feel the rush of revelation or joy right now. But in the quiet, God is still planting seeds. Faith isn't proved in the mountaintop—it's refined in the drought. Keep showing up. Keep opening His Word. Keep whispering those honest, weary prayers. Living water is coming.

Scripture

"For I will pour water on the thirsty land, and streams on the dry ground; I will pour out my Spirit…"
— Isaiah 44:3

"Blessed are those who hunger and thirst for righteousness, for they shall be filled."
— Matthew 5:6

"My soul thirsts for You, my flesh longs for You in a dry and weary land where there is no water."
— Psalm 63:1

Prayer

Lord, I feel distant from You. My spirit is dry and weary. I want to feel You again—to hear You, to know You're near. But even if I can't feel it, I choose to believe You are still with me. Revive my soul. Breathe fresh life into these dry bones. Stir up hunger where there's been apathy.

I surrender the pressure to perform and ask You to restore me in Your grace. Let my roots grow deep in this season, and when the time is right, let the rain fall again. In Jesus' name, Amen.

DAY 24

When You're Carrying Guilt

The Circumstance

You can't stop replaying it—the moment you failed, the word you wish you could take back, the decision that haunts you. Even after asking for forgiveness, guilt lingers. You wonder if you've really been forgiven, or if God is still disappointed in you. You carry it quietly, but it's heavy. *How could He still love me after that?*

Encouragement

Guilt may remind you of what happened, but grace reminds you of who God is. If you've brought it to Him in repentance, you are already forgiven. God doesn't forgive halfway. He doesn't hold it over your head. The cross was enough—once and for all. You don't have to carry what Jesus already carried for you.

Devotional Reflection

There's a difference between conviction and condemnation. Conviction comes from the Holy Spirit and draws you closer to God. Condemnation comes from the enemy and drives you into shame. Romans 8:1 is clear: *There is no condemnation for those in Christ.*

God isn't asking you to make up for what you did. He's asking you to receive what He's already done. Forgiveness is not about forgetting the past—it's about being free from its hold.

Even Paul, who once persecuted the church, could boldly say, *"I am what I am by the grace of God."* You can too. You don't have to prove your worth—you are covered in mercy. You don't have to keep punishing yourself—Jesus already paid the full price.

Scripture

"If we confess our sins, He is faithful and just to forgive us our sins and to cleanse us from all unrighteousness."
— 1 John 1:9

"Therefore, there is now no condemnation for those who are in Christ Jesus."
— Romans 8:1

"As far as the east is from the west, so far has He removed our transgressions from us."
— Psalm 103:12

Prayer

Jesus, I'm still carrying guilt You already paid for. Help me let go. Help me believe that Your forgiveness is real—and complete. I confess my sin and receive Your grace again. Silence the voice of shame. Remind me that I am not defined by my mistakes, but by Your mercy.

Wash me clean. Teach me how to live free. And when the past tries to whisper again, let Your truth shout louder: I am forgiven. I am redeemed. I am Yours. In Jesus' name, Amen.

DAY 25

When You're Under Spiritual Attack

The Circumstance

You're feeling crushed on every side. What should be minor feels overwhelming. Your thoughts are chaotic. Your sleep is disrupted. You're short-tempered, discouraged, or unusually fatigued. The people around you seem off. Your prayers feel blocked. And deep in your spirit, you know: *This is war.*

Encouragement

You are under attack because you are anointed, appointed, and advancing. The enemy doesn't waste ammo on those who pose no threat. But he's already defeated. His weapons may form—but they will not prosper. You are not fighting for victory—you are fighting from it. Your authority is blood-bought. Your armor is heavenly. Your standing is sure.

Devotional Reflection

Spiritual warfare is real—and often invisible. But God has not left you exposed. You have weapons that are not of this world, mighty through God to pull down strongholds. (2 Corinthians 10:4)

The enemy attacks your mind because he fears your calling. He stirs confusion because your clarity threatens him. He distracts you with drama because your focused obedience shakes kingdoms. But you are not alone, and you are not powerless.

Ephesians 6 commands you to *put on the full armor of God*—not once, but daily. The helmet guards your mind. The shield quenches every fiery dart. The sword—God's Word—cuts through every lie. When you feel surrounded, God has already encamped His angels around you.

Warfare is often the confirmation that you're moving in the right direction. Don't retreat. Worship louder. Pray harder. Speak Scripture boldly. Declare victory before you see it. You don't fight for approval—you fight because you've already been chosen.

You were born to overcome.

Scripture

"Finally, be strong in the Lord and in His mighty power. Put on the full armor of God, so that you can take your stand against the devil's schemes."
— Ephesians 6:10–11

"The weapons of our warfare are not carnal, but mighty in God for the pulling down of strongholds."
— 2 Corinthians 10:4 (NKJV)

"You are of God, little children, and have overcome them, because He who is in you is greater than he who is in the world."
— 1 John 4:4

"When the enemy comes in like a flood, the Spirit of the Lord shall lift up a standard against him."
— Isaiah 59:19

Prayer

Lord of Hosts, I feel the weight of this war, but I will not back down. I rise today in the full armor of God. I cover my mind with salvation, my heart with righteousness, my feet with peace, and my spirit with faith. I pick up the sword of the Spirit and declare truth over every lie.

I bind every spirit of fear, confusion, heaviness, distraction, and retaliation in Jesus' name. I cancel every demonic assignment sent against my life. I decree that no weapon formed against me shall prosper, and every tongue raised against me is condemned. Let Your fire surround me. Let angels be assigned to my household. Let victory break through. I belong to the Lord, and I fight from a place of triumph. In Jesus' name, Amen.

DAY 26

When You Need Peace in the Storm

The Circumstance

You didn't ask for this storm. You were just trying to obey God, do the right thing, stay faithful. But now life feels out of control. The phone call changed everything. The diagnosis dropped like lightning. The financial pressure won't let up. Or maybe it's just the slow buildup of stress, grief, and unspoken fear—and now it's too much.

You're praying, but still panicking. Trusting, but also trembling. Trying to be strong, but secretly wondering: *God, where are You in all this?*

Encouragement

You're not weak for feeling overwhelmed. You're not less spiritual because your faith is shaking. Even the disciples—men who walked with Jesus—cried out in fear during the storm. And what did Jesus do? He stood up, spoke peace, and reminded them He was with them the whole time.

That same Jesus is in your boat right now. You're not going under. He is the peace that holds when everything else is breaking.

Devotional Reflection

Sometimes the storm isn't a situation—it's internal. It's the war in your thoughts. The panic in your chest. The uncertainty in your future. You smile through it for others, but inside, you're just trying to make it to the next day. You're tired of pretending you're okay. You just want peace.

The world tells you peace comes when the storm ends. But God offers peace in the middle of it. Real peace. Not surface calm, but soul-deep stillness that defies explanation.

He may not snap His fingers and stop the storm today. But He can steady your spirit before the wind dies down. His peace isn't fragile. It's not based on outcomes. It's rooted in His presence—and He hasn't gone anywhere.

If all you can do is whisper His name, that's enough. If all you can do is sit in silence and cry, He's sitting with you. And when the storm finally passes, you'll know—He carried you through it.

Scripture

"He got up, rebuked the wind and said to the waves, 'Quiet! Be still!' Then the wind died down and it was completely calm."
— **Mark 4:39**

"You will keep in perfect peace those whose minds are steadfast, because they trust in You."
— **Isaiah 26:3**

"Even though I walk through the darkest valley, I will fear no evil, for You are with me."
— **Psalm 23:4**

Prayer

Jesus, this storm is too much for me. I don't have the answers. I don't feel strong. But I know You're here—even when I can't see what You're doing. I need Your peace—the kind that holds me together when everything else is falling apart.

Quiet the storm inside me. Guard my heart from fear. Wrap me in Your presence. Speak to my anxious thoughts. Teach me to breathe again, to trust again, to rest in You again. Even if nothing around me changes today, let peace rise within me. I believe You're not just in the storm— You're Lord over it. In Your name, Jesus, I receive Your peace. Amen.

DAY 27

When You're Believing for a Miracle

The Circumstance

You've tried everything. You've prayed, fasted, waited. You've asked others to agree with you in faith. And yet, the breakthrough hasn't come. The diagnosis hasn't changed. The child hasn't come home. The provision hasn't arrived. You're standing in faith, but also standing in the tension between hope and heartbreak. *God, are You still coming through for me?*

Encouragement

Miracles are not magic—they are manifestations of God's mercy and power. And He is still the same miracle-working God who parted seas, healed lepers, and raised the dead. Your situation may look impossible—but He specializes in impossibilities. The delay doesn't cancel the promise. And even if it tarries, He is still able.

Devotional Reflection

Believing for a miracle can be exhilarating—and exhausting. You feel full of faith one moment and filled with doubt the next. You see God move in others' lives, and wonder if He's skipped over you.

But throughout Scripture, we see that miracles often came after desperation, not before. The woman with the issue of blood pressed through the crowd. Blind Bartimaeus cried out louder. The paralytic's friends tore through a roof. Faith wasn't passive—

it was persistent.

So don't stop knocking. Don't stop praying. Don't let delayed answers convince you that God isn't listening. Sometimes the greatest miracle is what He does in you while you're waiting on the miracle you're asking for.

And even when you don't see it yet, He's moving behind the scenes, aligning heaven and earth on your behalf.

Scripture

"Jesus looked at them and said, 'With man this is impossible, but with God all things are possible.'"
— **Matthew 19:26**

"Blessed is she who has believed that the Lord would fulfill His promises to her."
— **Luke 1:45**

"Now to Him who is able to do exceedingly abundantly above all that we ask or think…"
— **Ephesians 3:20**

Prayer

Lord, I'm still believing. Even though it's been hard. Even though I've been disappointed. Even though I don't see the answer yet. I'm choosing to believe again today. I know You're able. I know You're faithful. I know You're not finished.

Strengthen my faith. Guard my heart from fear. Let hope rise again. I invite You to move in power—in Your way and Your timing. Whether You work through a whisper or a wonder, I trust You to do what only You can. I still believe in miracles… and I still believe in You. In Jesus' name, Amen.

DAY 28

When the Church Has Failed You

The Circumstance

You went to church to find God... and found judgment instead. You sought community and were met with cliques. You trusted leadership and were betrayed, silenced, overlooked, or even spiritually abused. The place that should have been safe became a source of pain. You still love Jesus, but you're wrestling with His people. *Can I really come back from this?*

Encouragement

God sees what happened to you—and He grieves it too. The failures of people do not reflect the faithfulness of Christ. The church may have wounded you, but Jesus never will. He is not distant from your pain. He is the Shepherd who gathers the bruised and binds up their wounds. Don't confuse the imperfection of people with the heart of the Savior.

Devotional Reflection

Some of the deepest wounds are spiritual ones—because they happen in the places you trusted most. It's disorienting when the body of Christ acts in a way that contradicts His love, His humility, and His truth.

But even Jesus was betrayed by one of His own. He was misunderstood by religious leaders, falsely accused by priests, abandoned by those closest to Him. He knows this pain intimately.

You don't have to ignore what happened. Healing doesn't require pretending. But it does require bringing the wound to the Healer. Let God deal with those who hurt you. Release them, not because they were right, but because you were never meant to carry the weight of their sin.

The church is broken because people are broken. But the true Church—the Bride of Christ—is still being made ready, washed in the Word, restored by His love. There is still beauty in the body. There are still shepherds who care, communities that love, and places where you can heal.

Don't give up on what God created, even if others have distorted it. He still has a place for you.

Scripture

"Woe to the shepherds who are destroying and scattering the sheep of my pasture!" declares the Lord.
— Jeremiah 23:1

"He heals the brokenhearted and binds up their wounds."
— Psalm 147:3

"Come to Me, all you who are weary and burdened, and I will give you rest."
— Matthew 11:28

Prayer

Jesus, I've been hurt by Your people, and my trust is bruised. I still love You, but I feel guarded, disappointed, and unsure how to move forward. Help me separate who You are from what they did. Heal my wounds, not just for my sake—but so I can worship and love again without fear.

Teach me to forgive, even when it's hard. Guide me to a place where I can grow and be safely rooted. And thank You, Jesus, for never failing me. Your love is still pure. Your arms are still open. Your presence is still home. In Your name, Amen.

DAY 29

When Pastors Have Disappointed You

The Circumstance

You respected them. You trusted their voice. You followed their leadership. But now you're carrying the weight of disappointment—maybe even betrayal. Perhaps it was moral failure, spiritual manipulation, hypocrisy, or neglect. Maybe it was just silence when you needed a shepherd's voice most. Whatever the details, the ache is real. You wonder, *If the one who led me faltered, can I trust again?*

Encouragement

God never asked you to put your faith in man. Your trust belongs to Him alone. Pastors are human—called, yes, but also flawed. When they fall short, it wounds deeply. But Jesus, the Great Shepherd, never fails. He never misleads. He never abuses His authority. And even when earthly shepherds disappoint, He still leads His sheep with gentleness and truth.

Devotional Reflection

Throughout Scripture, God holds spiritual leaders to high standards—and He grieves when they break trust. But He also reminds us that no person, title, or position holds the place of Christ. We honor pastors, but we do not worship them. We receive their leadership, but we build our foundation on Jesus.

When a pastor falls or fails, it can shake your faith. But that's when the roots are tested. If your faith was in the vessel, it may crack. But if your faith is in the Source, you will stand.

This doesn't mean your grief isn't valid. It is. God invites you to bring it all to Him—disillusionment, hurt, even anger. But don't let a leader's failure rob you of fellowship, or your calling, or your relationship with God. Don't walk away from Jesus because someone misrepresented Him.

Let God heal what people mishandled. Let Him restore what their failure fractured. And when you're ready, trust again—but only with your eyes fixed on the only perfect Shepherd.

Scripture

"Woe to the shepherds who destroy and scatter the sheep of My pasture!" says the Lord.
— Jeremiah 23:1

"I am the good shepherd. The good shepherd lays down his life for the sheep."
— John 10:11

"Fixing our eyes on Jesus, the author and perfecter of our faith…"
— Hebrews 12:2

Prayer

Jesus, I've been hurt by someone I looked up to—and I don't know what to do with this disappointment. I trusted them to lead me closer to You, but now I feel confused and wounded. Help me process this pain with You, not apart from You. Remind me that You are still my Shepherd, still good, still faithful.

Heal the part of me that wants to run or harden. Teach me to trust again—wisely, but without fear. Thank You for being everything no human leader ever could be. I place my eyes back on You. In Your name, Amen.

DAY 30

When You're Starting Over

The Circumstance

Everything has changed. Maybe it was your decision—or maybe it wasn't. A job ended. A marriage dissolved. A move, a loss, a closed door. Now you're staring at a blank page and wondering how to begin again. You feel the weight of what you lost and the fear of what's next. *God, how do I rebuild from here?*

Encouragement

Starting over is not failure—it's an invitation to something new. God isn't recycling your past. He's doing a new thing. And while it may feel like you're beginning from scratch, you're not starting from nothing—you're starting from grace. Every ending you've endured has prepared you for this beginning.

Devotional Reflection

Beginnings can be hard. They remind you of what ended. They strip away the familiar. They force you to depend on God in ways you didn't expect. But you're in good company. Abraham started over in a foreign land. Ruth started over in her grief. Paul started over after being blinded by truth. And Jesus met broken people over and over again and said, *"Go. Begin again."*

The most powerful stories in Scripture were born in seasons of starting over. So don't despise small beginnings. God builds miracles from the ashes of what was.

You don't have to have it all figured out. You don't need a five-year plan. You just need to be willing to take the next step—with Him. He goes before you, behind you, and within you. The same God who brought you through the last season is the One who will carry you into the new one.

Scripture

"Forget the former things; do not dwell on the past. See, I am doing a new thing!"
— Isaiah 43:18–19

"Though your beginning was small, your latter days will be very great."
— Job 8:7

"Being confident of this, that He who began a good work in you will carry it on to completion…"
— Philippians 1:6

Prayer

Lord, I'm stepping into something new—and I feel scared, unsteady, and unsure. I don't know what's ahead, but I know You're with me. Help me release the weight of the past and embrace this beginning without fear. Show me how to rebuild—not in my strength, but in Yours.

Breathe vision into the empty places. Plant hope in the soil of surrender. Walk with me step by step until the unfamiliar becomes home. Thank You for being the God of new beginnings. In Jesus' name, Amen.

DAY 31

When You Need to Remember Who You Are in Christ

The Circumstance

You've been through some things. Life tried to name you—broken, forgotten, unworthy, too much, not enough. The enemy whispered shame in your ear, and somewhere along the way, you stopped believing you were still chosen. You've walked through betrayal, silence, failure, and loss, and you're wondering: *Did something in me disqualify the call? Am I still who God says I am?*

Encouragement

Before the pain, before the shame, before the mistake, God had already called you by name. Your identity wasn't formed in the fire—it was forged in eternity. The struggle may have shaken you, but it didn't steal your sonship. The storm may have silenced your confidence, but it didn't cancel your crown. You are still chosen. Still His. Still called. Still covered.

Devotional Reflection

When God called Moses, he was hiding. When He chose David, he was overlooked. When He named Gideon a mighty warrior, Gideon was threshing wheat in fear. The point is not how strong you feel—it's what God has declared. And what He speaks over you is unchanging, unshakable truth.

You are more than the divorce. More than the bankruptcy. More than the addiction, the diagnosis, the silence, the layoff. You are not defined by the chapter you're in—you are defined by the One who authored your entire story.

Jesus didn't save you to make you a survivor. He saved you to make you a son. A daughter. An heir. A warrior. A witness. Heaven backs your identity. Hell fears it. And all of creation is groaning for the sons and daughters of God to rise and walk like they believe it.

Don't just remember who you are—start living like you know whose you are.

Scripture

"But you are a chosen people, a royal priesthood, a holy nation, God's special possession, that you may declare the praises of Him who called you out of darkness into His wonderful light."
— **1 Peter 2:9**

"For in Christ Jesus you are all children of God through faith."
— **Galatians 3:26**

"The Spirit you received brought about your adoption to sonship. And by Him we cry, 'Abba, Father.'"
— **Romans 8:15**

Prayer

Abba Father, remind me. Remind me who I am. Not what I've been through, not what they said, not what I lost—but what You declared before I ever breathed. I am Yours. I am known. I am chosen. I am called. I am seated in heavenly places with Christ.

Break every false label off of me. Restore every stolen piece of identity. Awaken the warrior in me again. Let me rise as the one You created before time began—marked by grace, anointed for purpose, clothed in righteousness. I am not what the enemy said. I am who You say. In Jesus' name, Amen.

BONUS DAY 1

When You Feel Invisible in Your Workplace

The Circumstance

You serve your country not with flags or parades, but with early mornings, policy briefs, reports, audits, inspections, and tenacity. You work in systems that can feel bureaucratic, political, slow to change—and quick to overlook. While others chase titles or recognition, you show up with quiet excellence, holding the line, mentoring others, and upholding standards.

And yet, you're passed over. Overworked. Dismissed. Unthanked. You carry a mission no one applauds. And you wonder, *Does any of this matter? Does anyone even know how much I carry behind this badge, desk, or ID card?*

Encouragement

Yes, it matters. And yes, God sees you. The One who placed you in that office, that command, that role—He has not missed a single act of faithfulness. While others may ignore your name, Heaven knows it well. God does not measure impact the way institutions do. He values integrity more than influence, consistency more than clout, and obedience more than applause.

You may be invisible to your leadership, but you are indispensable to the Kingdom. He planted you in that space not just for a paycheck—but for purpose.

Devotional Reflection

You are salt and light in a system that desperately needs both. When others cut corners, you raise the standard. When others turn a blind eye, you speak up. You represent the Kingdom of God in federal service, and that is no small calling.

You are not just doing your job—you are stewarding justice, equity, order, and accountability. You are interceding without words through every spreadsheet, site visit, memo, and meeting. God sees the late nights, the emails you didn't have to answer, the battles you fought for what was right—not popular.

And if no one ever gives you a coin, certificate, or ceremony, you will still receive a crown. Because your reward does not come from a GS level—it comes from the King of Kings, who keeps perfect records.

Scripture

"God is not unjust; He will not forget your work and the love you have shown Him as you have helped His people and continue to help them."
— Hebrews 6:10

"Serve wholeheartedly, as if you were serving the Lord, not people, because you know that the Lord will reward each one for whatever good they do..."
— Ephesians 6:7–8

"Promotion does not come from the east or the west, but from the Lord."
— Psalm 75:6–7 (paraphrased)

Prayer

Lord, You called me to serve—and I have, but lately it feels like I don't matter. Others rise while I'm left behind. Others take credit while I stay silent. But today, I bring this weariness to You. Remind me that my labor is not in vain. Remind me that You see what leadership may overlook.

Strengthen me to keep showing up with excellence. Let my witness be louder than politics. Let my work be worship. Elevate me in Your timing, and sustain me until then. I am not forgotten—I am assigned. And I will serve as unto You, the true and righteous Judge. In Jesus' name, Amen.

BONUS DAY 2

When Leadership Doesn't See Your Value

The Circumstance

You lead from where you stand. You've trained others, taken initiative, solved problems others ignored. You've stayed late, stepped up, and upheld the mission when others coasted. Yet leadership barely notices—or worse, they dismiss you entirely. No thank you. No advancement. No seat at the table. And deep down, it stings. *Why am I always seen as support, never seen as essential?*

Encouragement

The One who gave you your gifts never needs reminding of your worth. God saw your value before you ever earned a title, wrote a policy, or saved the day. Even when earthly leadership overlooks you, He is preparing you for something greater. He does not promote based on politics—but purpose.

You may be invisible to your boss, but you are handpicked by Heaven. What they don't see, God is recording. What they ignore, He is multiplying.

Devotional Reflection

Joseph was forgotten in prison by the cupbearer—but remembered by God. David was left out of the lineup—but called out by the prophet. Jesus was rejected by the temple elite—but anointed by God Himself. If you're being overlooked, you're in good company.

Leadership that fails to see your value cannot cancel your calling. It may delay recognition, but it cannot stop God's elevation. Sometimes He hides you to protect you. Sometimes He withholds titles to refine you. But in every season, He is positioning you for influence that's not dependent on man's approval.

Keep walking in integrity. Keep sowing in excellence. Let your work speak. Let your worship lead your mindset. And let God determine the time and place of your promotion. When He opens a door, no one can shut it—not even those who never saw you coming.

Scripture

"Do you see someone skilled in their work? They will serve before kings; they will not serve before officials of low rank."
— **Proverbs 22:29**

"For promotion comes neither from the east, nor from the west… but God is the Judge: He puts down one and sets up another."
— **Psalm 75:6–7**

"Humble yourselves, therefore, under God's mighty hand, that He may lift you up in due time."
— **1 Peter 5:6**

Prayer

Father, it's hard to give my best when it feels like no one sees it. I've worked in the shadows while others shine. I've served with excellence and received silence in return. But today, I shift my eyes back to You. You see. You know. You reward.

Teach me to serve with joy, even when honor doesn't follow. Remove bitterness, renew my strength, and remind me that no leader's blindness can block Your purpose. When the time is right, lift me in a way no one can deny. Until then, I'll keep showing up—with grace, grit, and confidence in You. In Jesus' name, Amen.

BONUS DAY 3

When You're Carrying More Than Your Share

The Circumstance

The task list never ends. You're covering for others—again. Projects land in your lap because "you're dependable." You're carrying your duties, cleaning up messes, and holding things together so the mission doesn't fall apart. Others clock out without concern. But you carry it home. *Why does it always fall on me? Who's carrying me?*

Encouragement

God sees not only your workload—but your heart behind it. You're not being punished for being faithful. You're being trusted. And while others may avoid the weight of responsibility, you're being shaped by it. Heaven records what no one else thanks you for. And God never asks you to carry anything without offering to carry you first.

Devotional Reflection

It's not just the work—it's the weight. The silent stress. The pressure to perform. The knowledge that if you don't do it, it won't get done right—or at all. You serve out of conviction, not convenience. You push through while others coast. And you're tired.

Even Moses hit a breaking point when he carried too much

alone. But God provided help—not just relief, but delegation. Jesus carried the weight of the world—yet still retreated to rest. You're not weak for being tired. You're human.

God doesn't want you burned out in service. He wants you balanced in grace. So speak up. Set boundaries. Say no when needed. Your worth is not in your workload. It's in your obedience. God honors faithfulness, not exhaustion.

And when you've done all you can, rest in this: He who called you is faithful. The weight may be heavy, but you're not carrying it alone.

Scripture

"Come to Me, all you who are weary and burdened, and I will give you rest."
— Matthew 11:28

"Cast your burden on the Lord, and He will sustain you; He will never permit the righteous to be moved."
— Psalm 55:22

"Be strong and do not give up, for your work will be rewarded."
— 2 Chronicles 15:7

Prayer

Lord, I'm carrying so much, and it's getting heavy. I've taken on more than my share—not just in tasks, but in responsibility, expectation, and silent sacrifice. I give it all back to You. Show me where to lay it down. Show me what's mine to carry and what's not.

Strengthen my body, renew my spirit, and remind me that You are my helper. You don't just assign work—you walk with me in it. Thank You for seeing every unseen effort and honoring what no one else affirms. I choose to carry this season with You, not alone. In Jesus' name, Amen.

BONUS DAY 4

When You're Tired of Fighting the System

The Circumstance

You're not trying to make waves—you're just trying to do what's right. But every improvement feels like a battle. Policies outweigh logic. Voices are silenced. Truth is uncomfortable. Corruption hides behind titles. You've tried to fix what's broken, but the system pushes back harder. *What's the point, Lord, if no one wants change?*

Encouragement

God called you *into* that system—not because it was easy, but because He trusted you to shine in hard places. You were placed there for purpose, not popularity. And even when you're weary from pushing against resistance, He is strengthening your resolve. You're not losing ground—you're holding it.

Devotional Reflection

The Bible is full of faithful men and women who stood for righteousness in flawed systems. Joseph served Pharaoh. Daniel served Babylon. Esther stood in the palace of Persia. They weren't outside the system—they were placed *in it* to influence from within.

You may not see results overnight. You may feel like a lone voice. But God is not asking you to fix everything—He's asking you to remain faithful where He's planted you.

You are not just a cog in a machine—you are a kingdom carrier. You are confronting compromise with courage. And every time you choose integrity over ease, you are pushing back darkness with light.

Don't let frustration become your filter. Let faith be your foundation. God may not change the whole system yet, but He is changing lives through your witness. Your resistance is not in vain. You are making more of a difference than you know.

Scripture

"Do not grow weary in doing good, for at the proper time you will reap a harvest if you do not give up."
— Galatians 6:9

"Have I not commanded you? Be strong and courageous. Do not be afraid... for the Lord your God will be with you wherever you go."
— Joshua 1:9

"You are the light of the world. A city set on a hill cannot be hidden."
— Matthew 5:14

Prayer

God, I'm tired of trying to do right in a place where wrong is often rewarded. I've fought for truth and justice, and it feels like I'm alone in the battle. But today, I realign my heart with You. Remind me why You sent me here. Strengthen me not just to survive—but to stand.

Help me to lead with wisdom, speak with grace, and walk in authority. Even if the system never changes, change me. Let me be a light that never goes out, a witness that never quits. I trust that You're working through me, even when I don't see it. In Jesus' name, Amen.

BONUS DAY 5

When You're Trying to Lead with Integrity in a Toxic Culture

The Circumstance

You've chosen the high road when others cut corners. You've spoken the truth when it cost you politically. You've protected your people when systems devalued them. And some days, it feels like integrity only isolates you. Coworkers gossip. Leadership retaliates. The environment is reactive, self-serving, and quietly corrosive. You lead anyway. But sometimes you wonder, *Is it even making a difference?*

Encouragement

You were not appointed by man—you were assigned by God. And when you lead with integrity, you reflect His image in a place that's forgotten what truth looks like. Every time you choose character over compromise, you're planting seeds of change—even if they grow slowly. Your integrity is not wasted. It is warfare.

Devotional Reflection

Integrity rarely makes you popular. But it makes you powerful. The kind of power that comes from heaven, not hierarchy. When Daniel was placed in high government under a pagan king, he didn't conform—he stood firm. His integrity got him thrown in a lion's den, but it also shut the mouths of lions and changed a nation.

You may not get applause. You may even face opposition. But God defends those who refuse to bend. And when you lead with humility, truth, and consistency, you create space for others to rise with you. You are not just surviving the culture—you are subverting it with Kingdom values.

Let your leadership be worship. Let your courage be contagious. Let your posture say, *I'm not here for approval—I'm here for impact.* God will bless what you build in obedience.

Scripture

"The integrity of the upright guides them, but the unfaithful are destroyed by their duplicity."
— Proverbs 11:3

"Whoever walks in integrity walks securely, but whoever takes crooked paths will be found out."
— Proverbs 10:9

"Let us not become weary in doing good, for at the proper time we will reap a harvest if we do not give up."
— Galatians 6:9

Prayer

God, I'm trying to lead with integrity in a place where compromise is rewarded and silence is safe. But I wasn't called to fit in—I was called to stand out. Strengthen me to lead well. Guard me from bitterness, pride, and burnout. Keep my motives pure. Let truth and grace mark every decision I make.

When I'm tired, remind me that You are my source. When I'm criticized, remind me that You are my covering. And when I feel alone, remind me that You are in the room with me. I choose character over comfort. I lead for Your glory, not my gain. In Jesus' name, Amen.

BONUS DAY 6

When You're Burdened by the Weight of Responsibility

The Circumstance

You're the one people depend on. The one who makes hard calls, solves hidden crises, signs off on critical decisions, and keeps your team afloat. You manage safety, morale, compliance, budgets, and deadlines—often without thanks. Everyone assumes you're strong because you carry it well. But inside, you feel the weight pressing down. *Lord, who carries the one who carries others?*

Encouragement

You were never meant to carry it all alone. Yes, you were called. Yes, you were appointed. But you were also invited—invited to cast every burden on the One who never grows weary. God isn't asking you to be unbreakable. He's asking you to lean on Him daily. You don't have to lead from exhaustion. You can lead from grace.

Devotional Reflection

Leadership is sacred—but it's heavy. Especially when you're leading with integrity in an environment that constantly pulls on your capacity and conscience. There's pressure to get it right, protect your team, stay mission-focused, and preserve your own peace. But God never called you to hold what only He can carry.

Even Jesus pulled away from the crowds to pray. Moses had to appoint help when the burden became too great. David found strength in the Lord when his own men turned against him. And you? You're allowed to rest. To pause. To reset. You don't have to prove your worth through performance. You prove your wisdom by knowing when to lean on God more than ever.

Let His strength be your strategy. Let His voice cut through the pressure. And when the load feels too heavy—remember, the weight you carry is still in the hands of the One who carries you.

Scripture

"Cast your burden on the Lord, and He will sustain you; He will never permit the righteous to be moved."
— **Psalm 55:22**

"Come to Me, all you who are weary and burdened, and I will give you rest."
— **Matthew 11:28**

"My grace is sufficient for you, for My power is made perfect in weakness."
— **2 Corinthians 12:9**

Prayer

Lord, the weight is real. People depend on me, and I feel the pressure to always be steady. But I bring this burden to You today—every decision, deadline, conflict, and concern. I give You the silent pressure I don't even speak about.

Strengthen my spirit where I've grown weary. Remind me that I'm not leading alone. Let Your wisdom fill my mind and Your peace anchor my heart. Help me lead with grace—not just for others, but for myself. I trust You to carry what I cannot. In Jesus' name, Amen.

BONUS DAY 7

When You Want to Quit but God Says Stay

The Circumstance

You've endured the dysfunction, absorbed the stress, and prayed through the resistance. You've looked for the exit, considered other jobs, even asked God to open a door—but He hasn't. And the longer you stay, the more drained you feel. You're not bitter, just tired. *Lord, why am I still here?*

Encouragement

Sometimes the greatest obedience is staying put. Not because it's easy—but because it's divine assignment. You may not see fruit yet, but you are planting seeds. You may not feel favor, but you are walking in faith. And your presence in that place is no accident—it's a call. God's silence is not His absence. And His delay is not denial.

Devotional Reflection

It would be easier to walk away than to keep showing up in a place that feels dry, toxic, or thankless. But in Scripture, the places of greatest discomfort were often the places of deepest refinement. Elijah wanted to run—but God said, *"Go back."* Paul longed to leave thorny places—but stayed to birth churches. Jesus, knowing what was ahead in Gethsemane, stayed in place and prayed.

There is power in staying—not to suffer in silence, but to be shaped for strength. God may not have released you yet because He's still working through you, and He's also working in you. Your endurance is not wasted. It's being recorded in heaven and felt in the spirit realm. You are the light in a hard place. You are the remnant. And yes, you are tired—but you are also chosen.

Don't confuse the weight of warfare with the absence of God. His grace is sufficient for this season—and when it's time to go, He will make it clear. Until then, stand your ground.

Scripture

"Let us not grow weary in doing good, for at the proper time we will reap a harvest if we do not give up."
— **Galatians 6:9**

"Be still before the Lord and wait patiently for Him…"
— **Psalm 37:7**

"You need to persevere so that when you have done the will of God, you will receive what He has promised."
— **Hebrews 10:36**

Prayer

God, I'm ready to quit. Everything in me wants to walk away—but I sense You're still asking me to stay. Help me surrender, not in defeat, but in faith. Strengthen me in the waiting. Show me the purpose behind this pause. And while I stay, let me serve with joy, integrity, and expectation.

Protect my heart from resentment. Guard my spirit from burnout. And remind me daily that obedience is never wasted. I don't just want to go —I want to be sent. So until You release me, I will remain faithful. In Jesus' name, Amen.

BONUS DAY 8

When You're Called to Serve but Long to Be Seen

The Circumstance

You were created to serve—and you've done it well. You've poured into others, stayed behind to clean up, stepped up when no one volunteered. You've stayed faithful in the shadows, never seeking recognition... but sometimes it hurts when no one sees you. You wonder, *Is it wrong to want to be noticed?*

Encouragement

It's not prideful to want to be seen—it's human. But what matters most is whose eyes you long to catch. God sees what man misses. He honors what others forget. And He calls you beloved—not because of what you do, but because of who you are. He sees your heart behind every humble act. And to Him, that's everything.

Devotional Reflection

The world rewards the loud, the visible, the self-promoting. But God builds His Kingdom on servants—the ones who wash feet, not just take platforms. You are part of a holy lineage: Ruth gleaned in obscurity. David worshiped in fields. Jesus wrapped a towel around His waist and served in silence before He ever ascended in glory.

But even Jesus, fully God and fully man, needed to hear the Father say, *"This is My beloved Son, in whom I am well pleased."* If He longed to be affirmed, it's okay if you do too.

Just remember this: being unseen by man doesn't mean being unknown by God. He sees. He remembers. He rewards. And in due season, the very place where you were hidden may become the platform for your testimony.

Scripture

"Your Father who sees what is done in secret will reward you."
— Matthew 6:4

"Whoever wants to become great among you must be your servant."
— Mark 10:43

"For God is not unjust; He will not forget your work and the love you have shown Him as you have helped His people."
— Hebrews 6:10

Prayer

Lord, I've served in the shadows, and I don't regret it. But sometimes I long to be seen, to be valued, to know that what I've done has made a difference. Remind me today that You have seen every sacrifice. You've counted every unnoticed moment. And You are the rewarder of the faithful.

Heal any wounds of invisibility. Uproot bitterness or comparison. Let me continue to serve with a pure heart—because You are worth it. And when the time comes, bring honor in Your way and in Your timing. Until then, I'll keep showing up. I'll keep serving. And I'll keep trusting You to see what others don't. In Jesus' name, Amen.

BONUS DAY 9

When You're Working Behind the Scenes but Making Kingdom Impact

The Circumstance

You're not on the stage. You don't wear the title. You don't make headlines or sit at the head of the table. But you're the one holding everything together—behind the spreadsheets, behind the systems, behind the strategies. You pray over decisions no one knows you influence. You show up early and stay late. You don't have visibility, but deep down, you hope your work still matters. *Am I doing more than just managing tasks? Am I building anything eternal?*

Encouragement

Yes—you are. God does not need you to be seen to use you. Your obedience in the background is moving things in the foreground of His Kingdom. While others chase influence, you've chosen impact. While others strive for position, you've chosen purpose. And Heaven is responding.

Devotional Reflection

The Kingdom of God is built on unseen hands and surrendered hearts. You are like the builders of Nehemiah's wall—repairing sections with diligence, even if your name never makes the scroll. You're like the women who followed Jesus—supporting the mission behind the scenes, yet rewarded with the first glimpse of His resurrection.

You're doing more than a job. You're making spiritual investments. Every task offered with excellence, every hour sown in service, every problem solved with integrity is part of your worship. And while others may see administration, paperwork, or logistics—God sees a laborer building eternity.

You don't have to have a platform to have power. You don't have to have a mic to carry spiritual weight. Your consistency is preaching a sermon louder than words.

Stay faithful. Stay focused. And know this: your reward will far outweigh your recognition.

Scripture

"Whatever you do, work at it with all your heart, as working for the Lord, not for human masters."
— **Colossians 3:23**

"The last will be first, and the first will be last."
— **Matthew 20:16**

"Each one should use whatever gift he has received to serve others, faithfully administering God's grace in its various forms."
— **1 Peter 4:10**

Prayer

Father, I may not be in the spotlight, but I know I am in Your will. When no one sees what I carry, You do. When no one celebrates what I accomplish, You do. Strengthen me to keep working behind the scenes with joy and purpose. Remind me that I'm not just doing tasks—I'm sowing into eternity.

Use my quiet faithfulness to shift atmospheres, influence outcomes, and bring glory to Your name. And when the enemy tempts me to believe it doesn't matter, speak truth louder than my doubts: I am building something eternal. In Jesus' name, Amen.

BONUS DAY 10

When You're Forced to Retire with an Uncertain Future

The Circumstance

You gave decades to the mission. You endured deployments, deadlines, and decisions that shaped lives and legacy. You stayed when others quit. You sacrificed when no one saw. And now, not by your own choosing, it's over. Retirement came faster than expected—or was pushed on you without honor or clarity. You're left with questions: *Who am I now? What does purpose look like on the other side of the badge?*

Encouragement

Your title may have changed, but your calling hasn't ended. Retirement is not rejection—it's redirection. God is not done writing your story. What looks like a closed chapter is actually the beginning of a new assignment. You are not being shelved. You are being sent.

Devotional Reflection

Transitions are hard—especially when they feel forced. The identity you've carried in service becomes so woven into your routine that its removal can feel like a personal unraveling. But this is not the end. It is a divine shift.

Moses didn't step into full purpose until after 40 years of wilderness. Anna didn't become a prophetess until her later years.

Abraham received a promise of legacy at 75. God doesn't retire vessels—He repositions them. And if He allowed this transition, He has already prepared what's next.

You may not wear a uniform or hold a government title anymore, but you still carry wisdom, authority, and anointing. What you've stewarded in silence, He will now multiply in new spaces. Rest if you must—but don't retreat. There is still fire in your bones and fruit in your hands.

Scripture

"Even to your old age and gray hairs I am He, I am He who will sustain you."
— Isaiah 46:4

"They will still bear fruit in old age, they will stay fresh and green."
— Psalm 92:14

"The gifts and the calling of God are irrevocable."
— Romans 11:29

Prayer

Father, I didn't expect this season to come like this. It feels abrupt, confusing, and a little painful. I miss the rhythm, the title, the purpose I used to feel. But today I surrender it all to You—my past, my future, and this unfamiliar in-between.

Speak life into what's next. Show me how to walk in legacy without limitation. Remind me that I'm still useful, still powerful, still chosen. Let this be a launching, not a loss. And let my latter days overflow with impact, joy, and grace. In Jesus' name, Amen.

EPILOGUE: YOU ARE STILL STANDING

If you've made it to this page, it means you didn't give up. You've walked through days of pain, grief, silence, pressure, and waiting—but here you are. Still standing. Still believing. Still becoming. And that, beloved, is a testimony all by itself.

This devotional was never meant to just hand you comfort—it was meant to awaken you to the truth that you are not alone, and you are not powerless. Every entry you've read is a reminder that your struggle does not disqualify your strength. It reveals it.

You've prayed through storms and asked questions that don't have easy answers. You've cried and clung to hope. You've wrestled with God—and like Jacob, you may walk away with a limp, but you also walk away with a blessing. You are different now. Deeper. Rooted. Dangerous to the darkness.

No matter what chapter of life you're in, one truth remains: God is faithful. He didn't leave you when it hurt. He didn't abandon you in the waiting. And He didn't change His mind about your purpose.

You are more than a survivor. You are a vessel of fire and oil. You are living proof that strength isn't the absence of struggle—it's the presence of God in the middle of it.

So take the prayers, the promises, and the scriptures with you. Speak them over your home. Your family. Your future. And when the next hard day comes—and it will—you'll be ready. Not because you're fearless, but because you've learned where to run when the storm hits.

Run to Jesus.

He's still your shelter. Still your strength. Still your source. And He's not done with you yet.

BIBLE STUDY COMPANION

Reflect, Respond, and Rise Stronger in God's Word

How to Use This Companion

Each set of questions is designed to help you:

- Reflect on what you read
- Engage more deeply with Scripture
- Hear God's voice personally
- Apply His truth practically

You can journal your answers, use them in a group study, or return to them when you need to re-center your faith.

Reflection for Any Devotional Day

1. What part of this devotional resonated most with your current season? Why?

(Write honestly. Don't edit your heart.)

2. What emotion did this day's reading stir in you—hope, conviction, peace, resistance? What do you think the Holy Spirit is revealing through that feeling?

(God speaks even through your discomfort.)

3. Which Scripture verse spoke most deeply to you? Rewrite it in your own words, as a personal promise from God to you.

(Let it become a declaration over your life.)

4. What is one truth from this devotional that you need to *remember*, one lie you need to *reject*, and one step you can *take* in faith?

- Remember:
- Reject:
- Respond:

5. Write a prayer or declaration of your own, using your answers as a guide.

(Speak it out loud. Your words carry power.)

Scripture Study Challenge
Each week, choose one of the verses from the devotionals and go deeper:

- Read it in 2–3 translations (e.g., NIV, ESV, The Message)
- Look up the original Hebrew/Greek words (use Blue Letter Bible or BibleHub)
- Ask: What was the context of this verse? Who was it written to? Why does it matter to me now?

Then ask:
What does this verse teach me about God's character?
What does it reveal about how He sees me?
How can I pray this verse over my situation today?

Group Discussion Questions
(Perfect for small groups, mentorship, or spiritual friendship)
- Which day hit you the hardest—and why?
- How has your view of struggle or suffering shifted after going through this book?
- What does "strength in Christ" look like practically in your life right now?
- What is God calling you to *release*? What is He calling you to *embrace*?
- How can you support someone else who is struggling now that you've walked through these truths?

A FINAL ENCOURAGEMENT

Every hard day you've faced was not just a trial—it was a training ground.

Let these truths move from your head to your heart, from your heart to your habits, and from your habits to your witness.

You are not just a reader of this book.
You are a warrior in the making.
And the Word of God is your sword.

Made in the USA
Coppell, TX
19 January 2026

68747796R00059